The Viking Library

Viking Gods and Legends

Andrea Hopkins, Ph.D.

The Rosen Publishing Group's

PowerKids Press™

New York

To the legendary Barbara Mercer. There never was a truer friend.

Published in 2002 by The Rosen Publishing Group, Inc.
29 East 21st Street, New York, NY 10010

First Edition

Book Design and Layout: Michael Caroleo

Project Editor: Frances E. Ruffin

Photo Credits: Cover page, title page and p. 19 (ship burning) © York Archaeological Trust; cover page, title page and p. 20 (Thor's hammer), 7, 15 (Thor) © Werner Forman Archive/Thjodminjasafn, Reykjavik, Iceland (National Museum); pp. 4 (ship painting), 19 (Viking funeral painting) © Mary Evans Picture Library; p. 4 (Tollund man) © Werner Forman Archive/Silkeborg Museum, Denmark; p. 16 (forge stone) © Werner Forman/CORBIS; pp. 7 (Freya), 20 (blacksmith mould) © Werner Forman/National Museum, Copenhagen; pp. 3, 15 (Freya pendant), 3, 8 (World Serpent brooch), 7 (Odin), 11 (funerary stones), 12 (Thor's hammer), 15 (tapestry) © Werner Forman Archive/Statens Historiska Museum; p. 8 © National Geographic Society; p. 11 (Odin lithograph) © Christel Gerstenberg/CORBIS; pp. 12 (both Thor images), 16 (Loki) © Bettmann/CORBIS; pp. 19 (burial place), 20 (Stave church) © Werner Forman Archive.

Hopkins, Andrea.
Viking gods and legends / Andrea Hopkins. — 1st ed.
 p. cm. — (The Viking library)
Includes index.
ISBN 0-8239-5814-0
1. Gods, Norse—Juvenile literature. 2. Mythology, Norse—Juvenile
literature. [1. Mythology, Norse.] I. Title. II. Series.
BL860 .H66 2002
293—dc21
                                                            00-012477

Manufactured in the United States of America

Contents

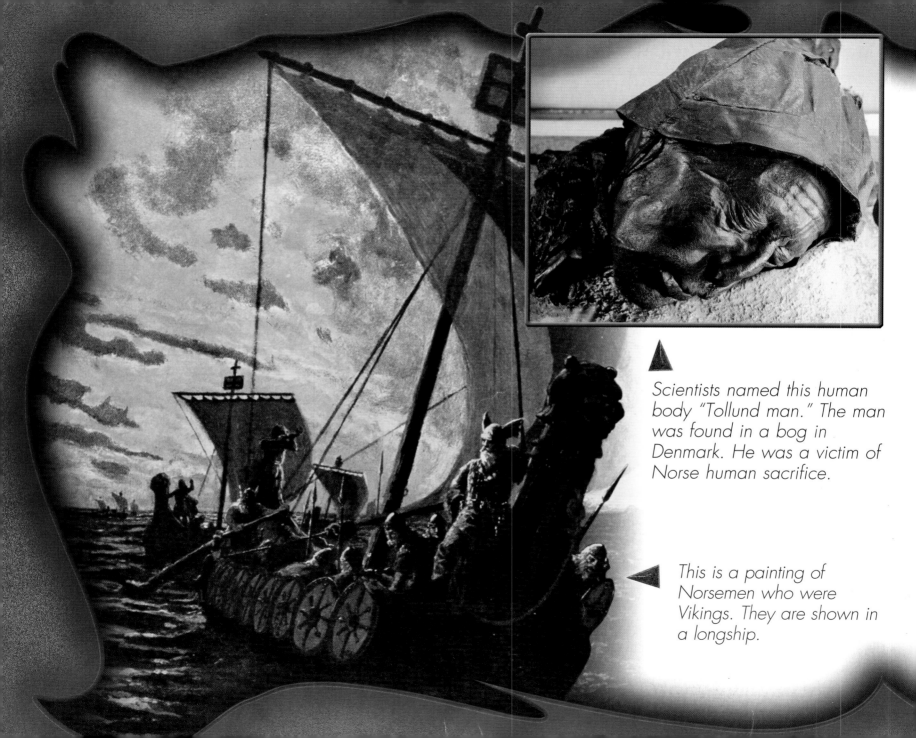

Scientists named this human body "Tollund man." The man was found in a bog in Denmark. He was a victim of Norse human sacrifice.

This is a painting of Norsemen who were Vikings. They are shown in a longship.

Viking Gods

Our word "god" was originally a Norse word. The Norse were people who lived in Norway, Sweden, and Denmark. Today those countries are called **Scandinavia**. Some Norsemen were Vikings. Vikings were people who sailed in longships to steal from people in other countries. Sometimes they traded with them. The Norse first became **Christians** around A.D. 1000. Before that, they were **pagan** and believed in many gods and goddesses. They worshiped mainly by **sacrifice**. To sacrifice means to give something valuable to a god. For the Norse, it meant offering jewelry or weapons. Sometimes it meant killing animals or even people.

The Norse believed that a sacrifice to their gods protected them from harm or made their crops grow. For Vikings, a sacrifice might keep their ships from sinking or give them victory in battle.

Learning About Norse Religion

   To honor or worship a god is how people practice a religion. Much of our information about how the Norse practiced their religion comes from things that **archaeologists** discover. We also learn about them from Icelandic **sagas** that describe pagan **legends** and **customs**. Around A.D. 1070, at the end of the pagan era, a German man named Adam of Bremen wrote about the Norse religion. He described a great temple that had been built in Uppsala, Sweden. The temple contained images of three Norse gods called Thor, Odin, and Frey. Adam based some of his writings on stories from Norse people that he had met in his travels. He probably made up the "great temple," however. Adam had never been to Uppsala. Archaeologists have never found a large temple there.

This is a bronze pendant of a woman who represents the Norse goddess Freya. It was made in Denmark.

This bronze pendant of the Norse god, Thor, was found in Iceland. It was made about A.D. 1000.

This bronze pendant represents Odin. He is wearing a horned helmet and is holding spears. It was made around the ninth century and was found in Sweden.

This bronze pendant of the awesome world serpent was found in Sweden and may have been been worn by a Norse chieftain.

The Norse Universe

In Norse legends, the **universe** existed in a giant ash-tree. The tree was named Yggdrasil. Midgard, the world of men, was in the center of the tree. Asgard, the home of the gods and the sky, was supported by branches that reached up through the world of men. Midgard was surrounded by a great ocean and icy, snowy mountains where the frost giants lived. They were the **ancient** enemies of the men and gods. Dwarves lived under rocks in the mountains. Elves and other spirits lived inside hills and valleys. Under the great ocean surrounding Midgard lay an awesome World Serpent. According to legends, this huge snake chewed away at the roots of Yggdrasil, the tree of the universe.

◀ *This photograph of the sea and mountains in Norway seems very much like the description of Midgard, the world of men in Norse legends.*

Odin

There were two **tribal** groups of gods in Norse legends. They were the Aesir and the Vanir. They lived together in Asgard, where each of them had his or her own splendid palaces that were called halls. They also had special weapons, **chariots**, and animals. Odin was the chief god of the Aesir. He was the god of conflict, the god of wisdom, and the god of poets. Odin rode a magical horse with eight legs, called Sleipnir. Odin's hall in Asgard was the most famous of all. It was called Valhalla, meaning the Hall of the Slain, for those who were killed in battle.

The large painting shows Odin on his throne in Valhalla. The funeral stone (top right) *shows Odin and his eight-legged horse, Sleipnir. The bottom stone shows the hunting and fighting at Valhalla.*

Thor

Thor was one of Odin's sons. He was very popular. More Norse people and places are named after Thor than any other god. He was the most important god for farmers and sailors. Legends say he lived in a palace that had 540 doors. His weapon was a great hammer, and he traveled in a chariot drawn by goats. The Norse believed that Thor controlled the weather. He could send fair winds for a sea voyage, and good weather for growing crops. His special power, however, was making violent thunderstorms. Thunder and lightning resulted whenever he struck blows with his huge hammer. Thor used his great strength to protect the world against giants.

At the left is an image of Thor with his goats, a painting of Thor's face, and a carving of Thor's hammer.

Other Gods and Spirits

Frigg was the wife of Odin and the mother of his sons Baldr and Hod. She was a strong goddess who sometimes disagreed with her husband Odin and occasionally outsmarted him.

According to Norse legends, many gods and goddesses lived in Asgard. Frey was the god of **fertility**. People made sacrifices to Frey at weddings. They hoped their offerings would bring children. Farmers hoped that Frey would make their crops grow. Frey's chariot was drawn by wild boar. Frey's sister Freya was the chief goddess of fertility and wealth. She was very beautiful and traveled in a chariot drawn by cats. She was also the chief of a group of female spirits called the Disir. They protected families and animals, and helped crops grow.

Norse gods and goddesses appear in many artifacts. The tapestry shows Odin, Thor, and Frey. His sister Freya is depicted in the pendant below.

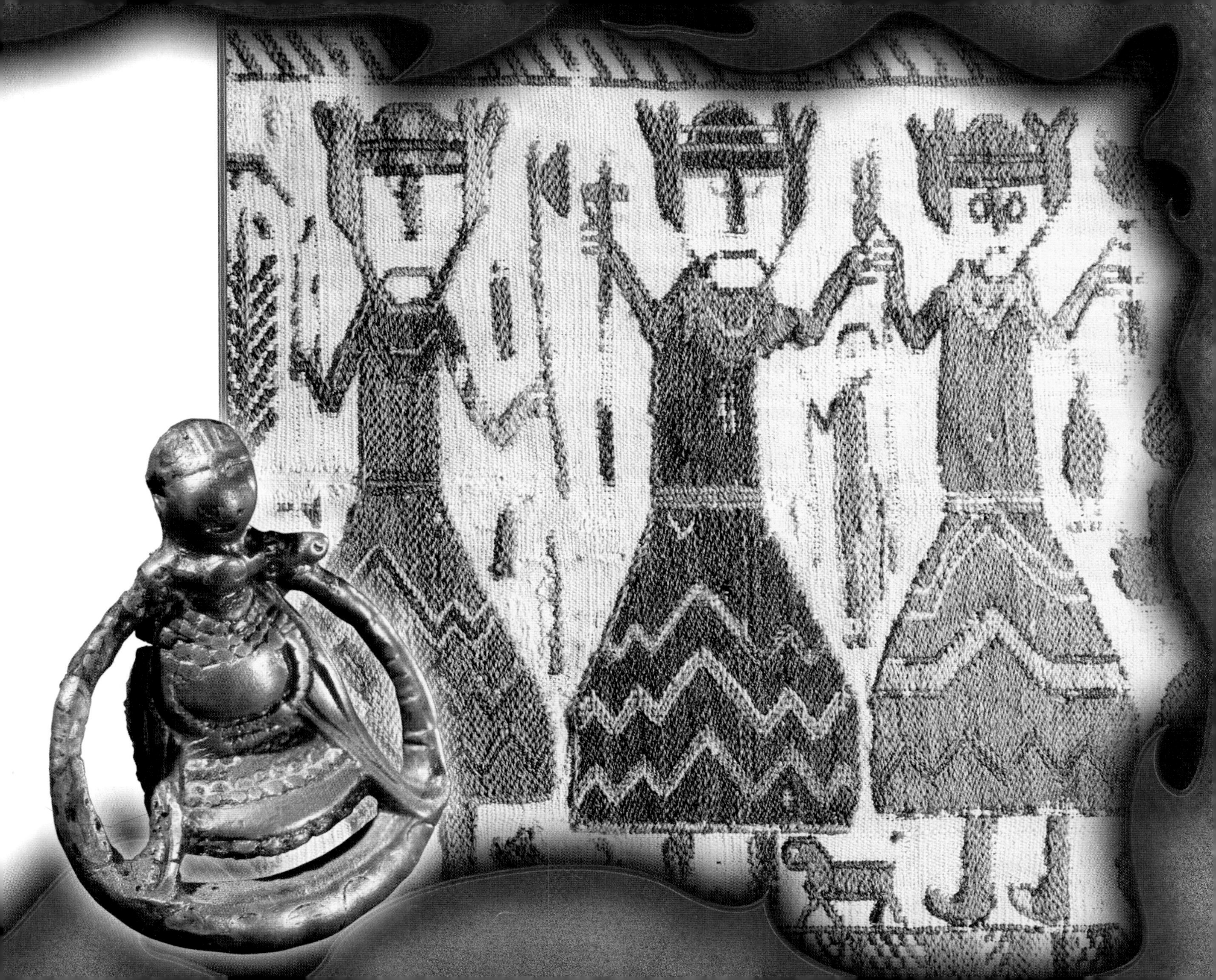

In this painting, Loki is shown captured and in chains. ▶

The stone shows the evil god Loki with his lips sewn together. ▼

Evil Loki

Nobody really knows from where Loki came. He was an evil god. It was said that one day he would destroy all of the Norse gods. He was clever and sly. Many legends tell of his deeds. Some were harmless tricks and others were cruel and dangerous. He could change himself into a woman or an animal. Odin knew that he would need to use all of his wisdom and tricks against Loki. Odin needed to prepare for the Day of Ragnarok. According to Norse legend, on this day the gods and their warriors would do battle against the giants and other monsters. This was the reason why Odin collected the souls of warriors killed in battle. They were to fight at his side.

Life After Death

We learn from Icelandic sagas that there was another good reason the dead were provided with everything they possibly could want in the next life. It prevented them from coming back!

It's very clear from Viking Age burials that Norse people believed in life after death. People were buried with food and drink, tools, weapons, clothes, jewelry, bedding, sleds, and sometimes even hunting dogs or horses. Occasionally human slaves were killed and buried with their masters. The Norse believed that the **afterlife** was pretty much the same as this life. Kings, queens, and great chieftains were buried inside real ships. These ships were burned or buried inside huge mounds of earth. The burial places were marked with rows of standing stones in the shape of a ship.

The background shows a Viking ship set ablaze.
Top Left: *There are 628 graves in this Viking burial mound in Denmark.*
Top Right: *This illustration shows a warrior king, his horse, and a ship set on fire and sent to sea.*

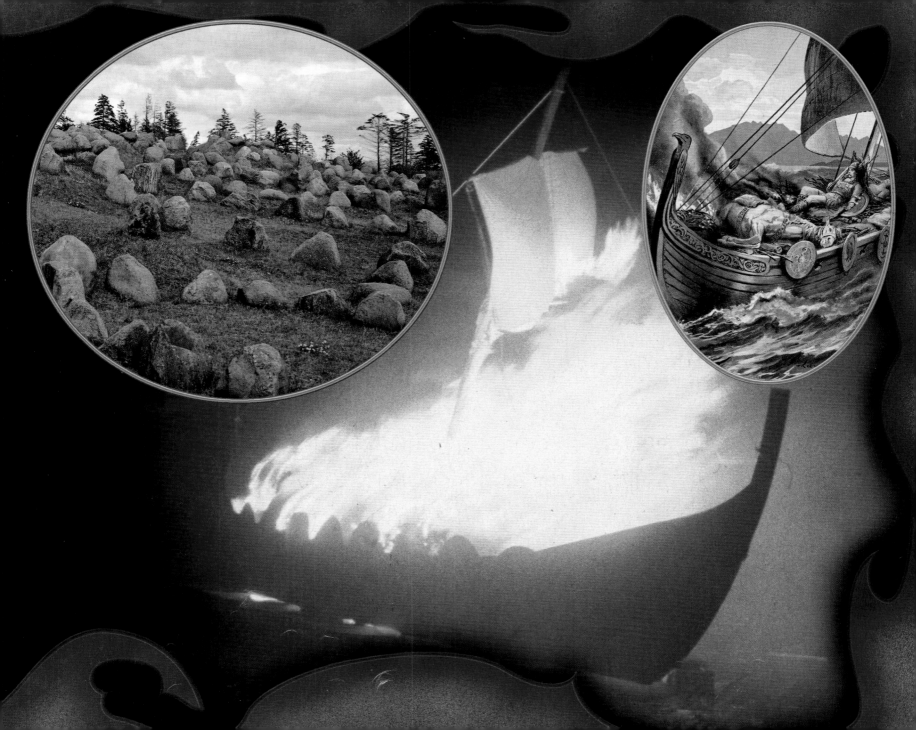

The image of ▶ Thor's hammer in the form of a cross shows that Christianity had an effect on its design.

A Norse metalworker's molds, in which molten metal was poured, has both Thor's hammer and Christian crosses.

▼

The Norse Become Christians

One result of the Viking Age was that during those centuries, Vikings learned a lot about Christianity when they raided or traded with other countries. By the end of the 900s, all of the European countries to the south and west of Scandinavia were Christian. The Norse were among the last pagans in Europe. The Vikings admired the wealth of Christianity and its splendid, large, stone churches. When they formed **settlements** in England, Ireland, Scotland, and Normandy (now part of France), they became Christians to fit in with their neighbors. Over the years, nearly all of the Norse people came to accept Christianity and its beliefs.

The photo shows a Stave church in Norway. Stave churches are believed to have been modeled after pagan temples.

The End of the Viking Age

By A.D. 1050, most Scandinavian kings had **converted** to Christianity. They also insisted that it become the main religion of their **subjects**. Christianity meant new rules for the Norse. They couldn't worship the old gods. They couldn't perform sacrifices or bury their dead in ships with valuable possessions. They had to go to church to worship. They couldn't marry more than one wife. They couldn't have Christian slaves. They could not burn down, rob, or commit murder in other people's churches. Many of the Norse who lived in the countryside stayed attached to their old customs and gods. It took a long time for everyone to agree to live by the new Christian rules. When that happened, it brought the end of the Viking Age.

Glossary

afterlife (AF-ter-lyf) Another life or world where people believe they will go after they die.

ancient (AYN-chent) Very old; from a long time ago.

archaeologists (ahr-key-AH-luh-jists) Scientists who study the buildings and artifacts of ancient peoples.

chariots (CHAR-ee-ots) Two-wheeled carriages pulled by animals, usually horses.

Christians (KRIS-chunz) People who follow the teachings of Jesus Christ and the Bible.

converted (kuhn-VER-tid) To have changed religious beliefs.

customs (KUS-tumz) The accepted, respected way of doing something that is passed down from parent to child.

fertility (fur-TIH-luh-tee) The state of being able to reproduce.

legends (LEH-jendz) Stories passed down through the years that many people believe.

pagan (PAY-gun) Someone who believes in many gods.

sacrifice (SA-krih-fys) To offer something to God as an act of worship.

sagas (SAH-guz) Stories about the history and experiences of a people.

Scandinavia (skan-dih-NAY-vee-uh) Northern Europe, usually Norway, Sweden, and Denmark.

settlements (SEH-tul-ments) Small villages or groups of homes.

subjects (SUHB-jekts) People who are ruled by a king or government.

tribal (TRY-buhl) Relating to groups of people who share the same customs, language, and ancestors.

universe (YOO-nih-vers) Everything that is around us.

Index

Web Sites

To learn more about the Viking gods and legends, check out these Web sites:
www.geocities.com/SouthBeach/Lagoon/7152/index2.html
www.merseygrid.co.uk/education/projects/myths/norse